DRAGO

ASHLEY GISH

INSECTS
X
BOOKS

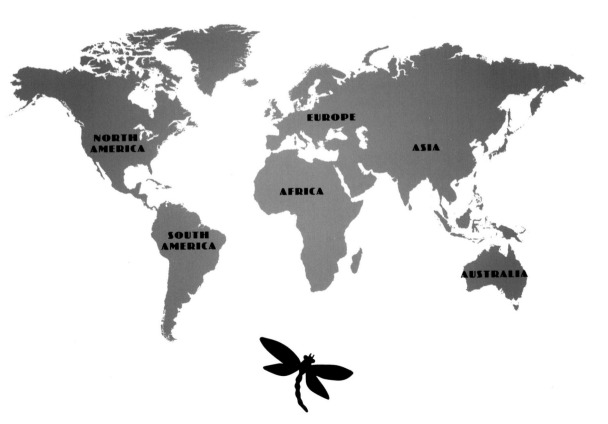

NORTH
AMERICA

EUROPE

ASIA

AFRICA

SOUTH
AMERICA

AUSTRALIA

CREATIVE EDUCATION · CREATIVE PAPERBACKS

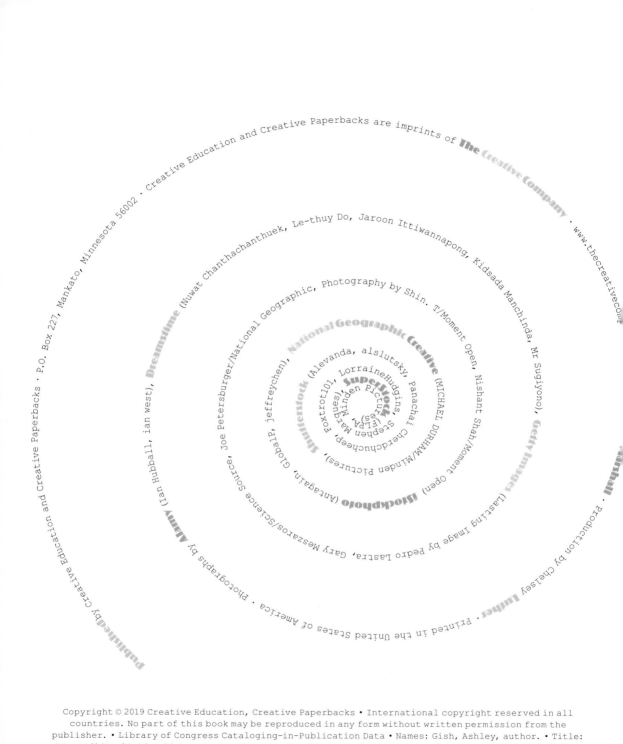

Creative Education and Creative Paperbacks are imprints of The Creative Company · www.thecreativecompany... · Published by Creative Education and Creative Paperbacks · P.O. Box 227, Mankato, Minnesota 56002 · Creative Education and Creative Paperbacks · Design and production by Chelsey Luther · Printed in the United States of America · Photographs by Alamy (Ian Hubball, ian west), Dreamstime (Niwat Chanthachanthuek, Le-thuy Do, Jaroon Ittiwannapong, Kidsada Manchinda, Mr Sugiyono), Getty Images (Lasting Image by Pedro Lastra, Gary Meszaros/Science Source, Joe Petersburger/National Geographic, Photography by Shin. T/Moment Open, Nishant Shah/Moment Open), iStockphoto (Antagain, GlobalP, jeffreychen), National Geographic Creative (MICHAEL DURHAM/Minden Pictures), Shutterstock (Alevanda, alslutsky, Panachai Cherdchucheep, Stephen Mcsween (FLPA), Minden Pictures), SuperStock (LorraineHudgins, Foxtrot101)

• Library of Congress Cataloging-in-Publication Data • Names: Gish, Ashley, author. • Title: Dragonflies / Ashley Gish. • Series: X-Books: Insects. • Includes index. • Summary: A countdown of five of the most fascinating dragonflies provides thrills as readers learn about the biological, social, and hunting characteristics of these powerful, flying insects • Identifiers: LCCN 2017060040 / ISBN 978-1-60818-991-5 (hardcover) / ISBN 978-1-62832-618-5 (pbk) / ISBN 978-1-64000-092-6 (eBook) • Subjects: LCSH: Dragonflies—Juvenile literature. • Classification: LCC QL520 .G4945 2018 / DDC 595.7/33—dc23
CCSS: RI.3.1-8; RI.4.1-5, 7; RI.5.1-3, 8; RI.6.1-2, 4, 7; RH.6-8.3-8
First Edition HC 9 8 7 6 5 4 3 2 1 • First Edition PBK 9 8 7 6 5 4 3 2 1

DRAGONFLIES

CONTENTS

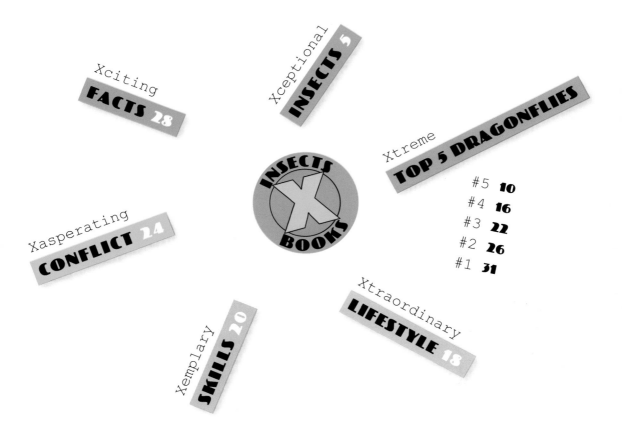

Insects X Books

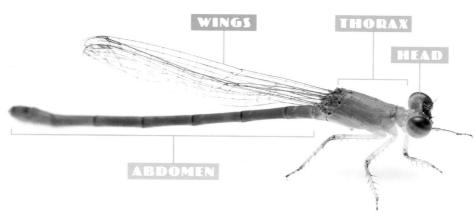

WINGS THORAX HEAD ABDOMEN

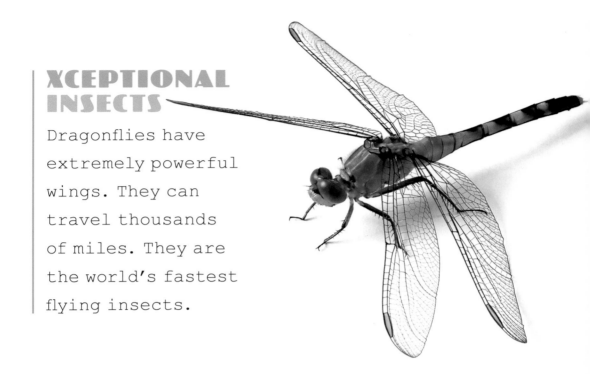

XCEPTIONAL INSECTS

Dragonflies have extremely powerful wings. They can travel thousands of miles. They are the world's fastest flying insects.

Dragonfly Basics

Dragonflies are insects. Like all insects, dragonflies have six legs. Their bodies consist of a head, a thorax, and an abdomen. All insects also have **antennae**. Dragonflies' antennae are short. Dragonflies have no bones. Their long, sticklike bodies are covered by an exoskeleton. This hard armor protects their bodies.

Dragonflies have two pairs of strong but flexible wings. The wings have many veins, but they are smooth. Dragonflies cannot close their wings like butterflies can or fold them up like beetles do. The wings have a thin covering of chitin (*KY-tin*). This is also found in exoskeletons.

DRAGONFLIES OF THE WORLD

More than 3,000 types of dragonflies exist around the world. They need to live near water to survive.

BLUE DASHER

FOUR-SPOTTED SKIMMER

EASTERN PONDHAWK

GLOBE SKIMMER

SCARLET DWARF

GIANT PETALTAIL

LARGEST VS. SMALLEST

Giant petaltails, whose wings span about 6.3 inches (16 cm) and body lengths 4.9 inches (12.4 cm), are the largest dragonflies. The scarlet dwarf's wingspan is only 0.75 inch (1.9 cm)!

GLOBE SKIMMERS' MIGRATION

Globe skimmers are world travelers. Researchers have found that these dragonflies travel from India to Africa. They glide on air currents to cross the ocean. This might be just one part of an even longer journey.

India

Africa

DRAGONFLY EYES

Each eye has about 30,000 tiny panels. These panels are called ommatidia (*ah-ma-TID-ee-uh*). Dragonflies can see in every direction except right behind them.

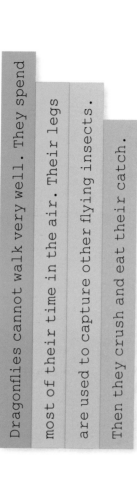

Dragonflies cannot walk very well. They spend most of their time in the air. Their legs are used to capture other flying insects. Then they crush and eat their catch.

Dragonflies mostly eat food caught in flight.

DRAGONFLY DIET

Each wing moves separately. This lets the dragonfly hover like a helicopter. It can move up, down, forward, backward, and sideways. Dragonflies can change direction in an instant. They can even fly upside down!

Most dragonflies live near freshwater sources.

FRESH WATER HOMES

DRAGONFLY BASICS FACT

To fly, dragonflies beat their wings about 30 times a second.

TOP FIVE XTREME DRAGONFLIES

Xtreme Dragonfly #5

Smallest Dragonfly The scarlet dwarf is the world's smallest dragonfly. Its wingspan is only three-quarters of an inch (1.9 cm). These dragonflies are named for the males' coloration. Males are bright red with black legs. Females are black with brown and green markings. Scarlet dwarfs live in Southeast Asia. They have also been spotted in parts of Australia. They are also called tiny dragonflies and northern pygmyflies.

Most male and female dragonflies are the same size. But males usually have brighter colors.

Dragonfly Babies

Female dragonflies lay eggs on water plants. Sometimes they drop their eggs into the water. The eggs hatch in about one week. Baby dragonflies are called nymphs. They live underwater. Nymphs shed their exoskeleton up to 15 times as they grow. This is called molting.

Dragonfly nymphs are fierce hunters. Their mouthpart has toothlike structures. It is called a labium. Nymphs can shoot their labium forward to nab **prey**. They eat mosquito **larvae**, small fish, and tadpoles. To swim, the nymphs shoot water through their rear ends.

After some time, nymphs become adult dragonflies. In smaller **species**, this happens within a few months. Larger species can take up to six years to change. At night, they stick their heads out of the water. They begin to breathe air. Then they climb up the stem of a water plant. They molt for the last time. Now they have wings. Adult dragonflies do not live long. They die soon after mating and laying eggs.

1 to 2 weeks
Eggs hatch

2 months / **6 years**
Nymphs live underwater

up to 15 times
Exoskeletons are shed

1 to 6 months

Teneral adults emerge

Adults mate before dying

When a nymph first emerges from its final molt, its body and wings are soft. It is called a teneral until its body hardens.

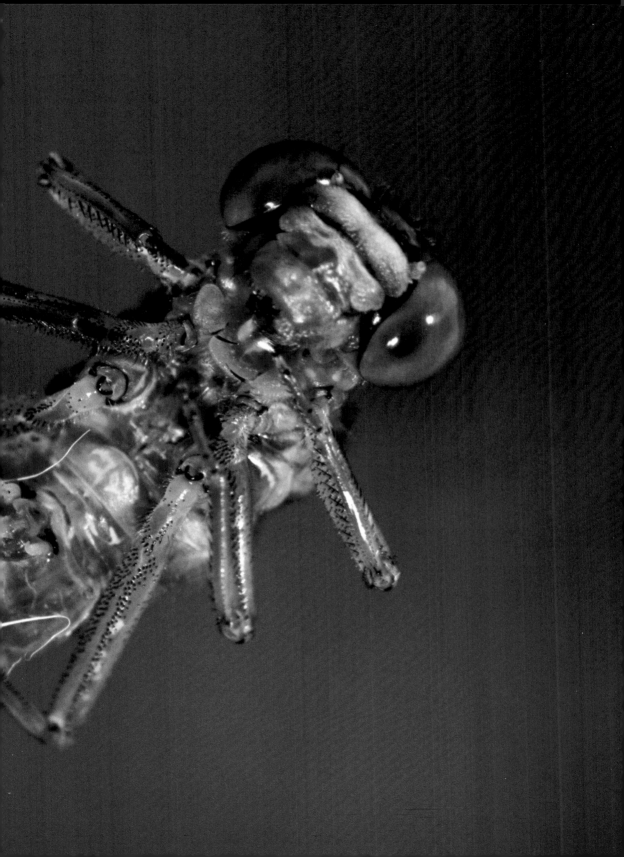

TOP FIVE XTREME DRAGONFLIES

Xtreme Dragonfly #4

Tasty Treats Eastern pondhawk dragonflies are common in Louisiana. And people eat them! Zack Lemann is an insect scientist. He works at the Audubon Butterfly Garden and Insectarium in New Orleans. He tells visitors how to cook dragonflies. First, dip them in raw egg. Then roll them in seasoned corn flour. Fry them in hot oil for a few seconds. Eat them with mushrooms and mustard butter. Eastern pondhawks taste like crabmeat!

XTRAORDINARY LIFESTYLE

Some dragonflies are fighters. Some are friendly. Dragonflies can move like no other insect. They can do handstands. They can skim the water like little jet airplanes.

Dragonfly hunting prey

10%

90%

successful attempts

misses

DRAGONFLY SOCIETY FACT

Dragonflies are in the scientific order Odonata. This name comes from th

Latin word for "tooth." It refers to a dragonfly's mouthpart.

Seaside dragonlet nymphs live in salt water.

SALTWATER DRAGONLETS

Dragonfly Society

Some dragonflies live only a few months. Others live for more than a year. Male dragonflies may guard their hunting areas. They fight with other males over their homes. They do this to attract mates. Females prefer partners with good hunting areas.

When the weather is warm, hundreds or even millions of dragonflies may gather together. These groups are called swarms. Scientists are not sure why dragonflies form swarms. Perhaps it is to eat at a plentiful food source. Swarms also travel together. Such travel is called migration.

In North America, dragonflies migrate north in summer. Their offspring migrate south in winter. Dragonflies called globe skimmers live around the world. Those that live in India travel great distances. In August, they migrate to Africa. Then, in December, they return to India. They cover 11,000 miles (17,703 km) round-trip!

XEMPLARY SKILLS

A dragonfly will eat any creature smaller than itself. It catches prey while flying. But it does not chase its prey down.

Darner dragonflies have long, thin bodies.

They look like long sewing needles called darning needles.

The females have sharp tails.

They cut tiny slits in plant stems.

Then they lay eggs inside the slits.

Dragonflies are smart. They watch where their prey is going. Then they go there, too. They are like football players running to catch a football thrown downfield.

Dragonflies grab prey with their feet. They bend their legs to make a cage. Then they bite the prey's head. They strip off its wings. Sometimes they land to eat. Their mouths can open as wide as their heads. Strong jaws turn prey to mush. Dragonflies sometimes get caught in spiderwebs. They have been known to fight spiders and win!

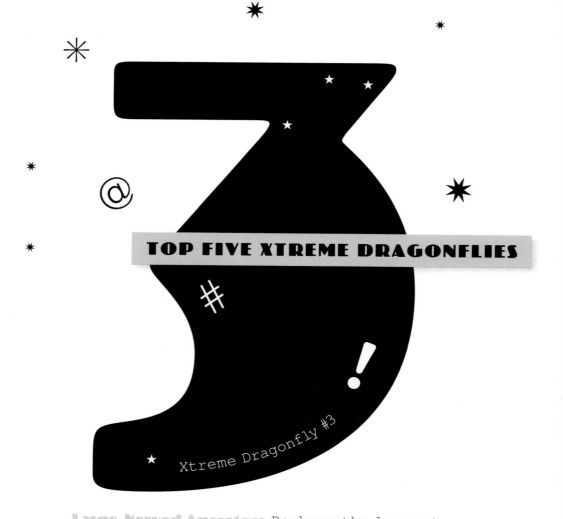

TOP FIVE XTREME DRAGONFLIES

Xtreme Dragonfly #3

Large-Nerved Ancestors Perhaps the largest insects that ever lived were dragonfly **ancestors** called *Meganeura*. They lived about 300 million years ago. Each wing was 13 inches (33 cm) long. That is about as tall as a milk carton! Their bodies were almost 24 inches (61 cm) long and as thick as a broom handle. *Meganeura* fossils have been found in France and England.

XASPERATING CONFLICT

Water pollution is deadly to dragonflies. Substances sprayed on farmland and lawns contain poisons. These poisons often end up in ponds and streams. People must take care of Earth's water to help dragonflies survive.

Dragonfly Survival

In the morning, dragonflies stretch out in the sun to warm up. To avoid overheating, they stand on their front two feet with their tails pointed straight up. This cuts down on the amount of sun hitting their bodies. Dragonflies also skim over water, touching it lightly. This cools them down and keeps their bodies moist. Too much heat can kill a dragonfly.

Climate change is slowly warming the planet. Scientists have recently learned that dragonflies seem to be changing, too. Many species' colors are lightening. Sunlight bounces off light-colored objects. Their new coloring will help dragonflies avoid overheating.

More than 450 dragonfly species are found in the United States and Canada. About 100 different species live in deserts. The Mojave Desert is the driest desert in the U.S. Variegated meadowhawk and brimstone clubtail dragonflies live there. It can be up to 120 °F (48.9 °C)! They live near slow-moving streams and rivers.

DRAGONFLY SURVIVAL FACT

Autumn meadowhawks do not mind cool weather.

Sometimes they do not migrate south until December or January.

Xtreme Dragonfly #2

Frequent Fliers The globe skimmer is a powerful dragonfly. It flies farther than any other insect in the world. It has broad wings. It can glide on the wind like a sailing ship. Globe skimmers travel across the Indian Ocean from Asia to Africa. They may stop at islands along the way to mate and lay eggs. Their offspring hatch and return to Asia. These dragonflies can travel more than 11,000 miles (17,703 km) in their lives.

Dragonflies are not dangerous.
They do not sting like bees. They rarely bite humans.

Common dragonfly nicknames include water
dippers and devil's darning needles.

The four-spotted skimmer is Alaska's state insect.
The green darner is Washington's state insect.

Damselflies are dragonfly relatives.
They are smaller and slimmer than dragonflies.

Females can lay up to 1,500 eggs at once.
They can lay several batches each year.

Each dragonfly species has tiny variations in body shape.
This keeps different species from mating with each other.

Dragonfly nymphs are also called naiads (*NAY-adz*). They are
named for the water fairies in ancient Greek stories.

Nymphs can take two months to six years to
become adults. This varies by species.

The Dragonfly Sanctuary Pond in Albuquerque, New Mexico, opened in 200

The biggest dragonfly in North America is the giant darner

The Hine's emerald dragonfly is at risk of dying out.
There are not many left in North America.

If a dragonfly cannot fly, it will starve.

In China, the dragonfly is nicknamed "old glassy"
because of its clear wings.

Blue dashers, four-spotte

skimmers, and wandering perchers are found as far north as Canada's Newfoundland and Labrador.

Xtreme Dragonfly #1

Largest Dragonfly The giant petaltail is the largest living dragonfly. It is found only in Queensland, Australia. It has a wingspan of more than six inches (15.2 cm). Its thick body can be nearly five inches (12.7 cm) long. Two smaller relatives, the black petaltail and gray petaltail (left), live in North America. Petaltail dragonfly nymphs live in moist burrows or under wet leaves on the water's edge. They hunt passing prey.

GLOSSARY

ancestors – early types of animals or plants from which later individuals developed

antennae – body parts that protrude from the head and are used for sensing surroundings

larvae – the newly hatched form of many insects before they become adults

prey – animals that are hunted and eaten by other animals

species – a group of living beings that are closely related

RESOURCES

Cooper, Ann. *Dragonflies Q&A Guide: Fascinating Facts about Their Life in the Wild*. Mechanicsburg, Pa.: Stackpole Books, 2014.

"Dragonfly." Bug Facts. http://www.bugfacts.net/dragonfly.php.

Sabet-Peyman, Jason. "Introduction to the Odonata: Dragonflies and Damselflies." University of California Museum of Paleontology. http://www.ucmp.berkeley.edu/arthropoda/uniramia/odonatoida.html.

van Dokkum, Pieter. *Dragonflies*. New Haven, Conn.: Yale University Press, 2015.

INDEX

Dragonfly lawar is a traditional Indonesian dish made with coconut, green beans, spices, and dragonflies.